The College Experience for Student Athletes

Amy Baldwin
Pulaski Technical College

Brian Tietje
California Polytechnic State University, San Luis Obispo

Shannon Stephens
California Polytechnic State University

PEARSON

Boston • Columbus • Indianapolis • New York • San Francisco • Upper Saddle River
Amsterdam • Cape Town • Dubai • London • Madrid • Milan • Munich • Paris • Montréal • Toronto
Delhi • Mexico City • São Paulo • Sydney • Hong Kong • Seoul • Singapore • Taipei • Tokyo

Editor-in-Chief: Jodi McPherson
Acquisitions Editor: Katie Mahan
Editorial Assistant: Erin Carreiro
Development Editor: Elana Dolberg
Senior Managing Editor: Karen Wernholm
Senior Author Support/Technology Specialist: Joe Vetere
Senior Production Project Manager: Kathleen A. Manley
Executive Marketing Manager: Amy Judd
Senior Procurement Specialist: Megan Cochran
Image Manager: Rachel Youdelman
Permissions Manager: Cheryl Besenjak
Permissions Project Manager: Pam Foley
Text Design and Production Coordination: Electronic Publishing Services Inc.
Composition and Illustration: Jouve
Cover Designer: Diane Lorenzo
Cover Photo: DAJ/Amana Images, Inc./Alamy

Photo credits: p. 1: Fotolia; p. 5: Fotolia; p. 7: Fotolia; p. 9: Fotolia; p. 12: Ljupco
Smokovski/Fotolia; p. 14: Godfer/Fotolia; p. 21: Jason Stitt/Fotolia; p. 25: Gert Vrey/
Fotolia; p. 29: Denlitya/Fotolia

Many of the designations used by manufacturers and sellers to distinguish their products
are claimed as trademarks. Where those designations appear in this book, and Pearson
Education was aware of a trademark claim, the designations have been printed in initial
caps or all caps.

10 9 8 7 6 5 4 3 2 1—CRK—16 15 14 13 12

www.pearsonhighered.com

ISBN-13: 978-0-321-87752-9
ISBN-10: 0-321-87752-7

1 The College Experience for Student Athletes

YOU ALREADY HAVE MAD GAME

Many student-athletes think of themselves as not being great students because they have put so much time and effort into their sport—time and effort that has been taken away from their studies. Athletes are constantly striving for success and want to get better, but rarely do they stop and think about the positive qualities that have already gotten them to where they are athletically. Here are a few qualities that should make you very proud of your own accomplishments.

You are obviously *hard working*. How else have you become a student-athlete at a university or college? You have been given some natural ability, but you have had to work to perfect that ability. With your ability and hard work you are accomplishing something that few others have been able to do: You are a collegiate athlete! According to the NCAA, only 3.5% of high school athletes go on to compete at the NCAA level (www.collegesportsscholarships.com). These percentages are similar for NAIA and community college athletes as well. You have accomplished quite a feat and you should be proud. Your hard work has allowed you to chase your passion.

Take a moment to reflect back on all the hours you have spent perfecting your craft: the practices during the week, the hours of games and travel, the time in the weight room, and all of the other hours that you have put into your sport. You must be *passionate* about your sport to continue to do this—or you just have mad talent. If you just have mad talent, think about how good you might be if you were to put in more time and effort.

You may not think you do, but you must have some *time management* skills. Sports are a balancing act. Getting to practice and games on time, remaining eligible in high school by completing the necessary academic requirements, conditioning, going to team meetings, lifting weights, and breaking down film, not to mention the actual games or competitions themselves, all require time management.

In order to be a quality athlete you have to be *persistent*. No student-athlete has succeeded without pushing through some tough times. Remember double days! Surely, you have lost some games. You are obviously still competing, so you did not give up, roll over, or let it shatter your ability to compete. You shook it off and came back the next day to compete again. Certainly, you have been injured. Minor or major injuries plague all athletes at some time in their career, yet you have continued to work through the pain because this sport means more to you than the injury itself. If you have practiced through injuries, you have also competed through pain and injury. This is just what athletes do—they persist. Have you had surgery or know other athletes that have had surgery? The answer is most likely yes, yet you are still competing. Remember those famous phrases from your coaches when you get hurt:

"It's just a little pain; you will work through it."

"Just throw some dirt on it."

"It's not going to kill you."

"That which does not kill you only makes you stronger."

"Just suck it up."

"Your team is counting on you!"

"We are going to need a trainer over here."

These phrases are meant to motivate you and help you understand that your body is capable of some extraordinary things. Or your coach didn't think you were really hurt and was challenging your commitment. Either way, you got back up and continued to compete.

Becoming a premier athlete does not happen without *dedication*. Without dedication there is no hard work or persistence. It would be very easy to just say "this is too tough" and quit, but there is something that does not allow you to do that. There is something that drives you through those tough times and all the traveling. Something that makes you go to practice even though you don't want to that particular day. Something has made you sacrifice family vacations, free weekends, video games at 3:00 P.M., and many other interests. Believe it or not, you are dedicated to your craft.

Successful athletes also possess *self-confidence*. You may lack this in other areas of your life, but without some self-confidence you would not be competing at the collegiate level. You must have some idea that you are pretty darn good to be where you are. You certainly don't doubt your abilities when you are winning. There is a level of trust that the work you have put in will pay off. Many athletes believe that they are better than their opponent. How else are you going to kick their (insert your own word here) when you compete against them? Self-confidence is a good thing, and you have it. One caution: do not mistake self-confidence for arrogance. In the collegiate setting, arrogance can hurt you in building great relationships that will help you succeed; self-confidence will not. This will be revisited in the communication section.

Student-athletes work effectively with a team and individually. You have to have self-motivation in order to excel in your sport. If you are competing with teammates, then you are only as good your weakest link. The goal of any team or individual is to win. You must push yourself and your team to accomplish this common goal. Think about this: is everyone on your team your best friend? Probably not, but when you hop on the field of play, you are all working together to accomplish one goal. To accomplish this goal, every person has to be doing their part. Do you high five every teammate after a win? Of course you do, because the team victory was bigger and more important than the differences you may have with an individual. For those of you competing in individual sports, your success or failure could dictate the outcome of the team, so you strive to do your best for yourself and for your team.

Riddle me this, league champions: are you not constantly working to get stronger and faster? Of course you are, because athletes are *constantly striving for success* and always motivated to get better. Most athletes are never satisfied and constantly strive to improve times, distance, accuracy, and power. So what if you won the league championship this year? You are happy for a little while and then you are ready to get back to work and win another championship the next year, to create a legacy. Surely you have had a few defeats, but this simply motivates you to get better. You would not keep returning to something if you were not motivated to succeed.

You have some *leadership qualities* as well. Were you a team captain in high school? Have you told teammates they have done a good job? Have you told them they need to do better? Led a team talk before a big game? Have you led by example? Motivated teammates? Helped an injured player off the field? Congratulated the other team on a job well done? Evaluated your own performance on the field of play? If you answered yes to any of these questions, then you have exhibited some leadership qualities. Leadership qualities are inherent to most athletes and are sometimes taken for granted. Pay attention to these qualities and be proud of yourself for having them. You are a natural leader in some capacity.

Athletes exhibit *physical and emotional endurance* at several points throughout their career. You cannot be a successful athlete without going through some tough times and working through it. In football and other sports, there is generally a week or so where you are put through "double days," or days when you practice twice. They can be very mentally and physically challenging to the body. Certainly you have experienced days when your body just does not want to cooperate with practice and your coach says "on the line" for some more conditioning. As you know, it is not uncommon for athletes to experience concussions, broken bones, and surgeries. Yet you have continued to push your body and mind beyond what many people think is possible. This is a quality that will stay with you for a lifetime. You should be proud of yourself; acknowledge and celebrate that you have this quality. There are not many people that are willing to fight through such physical and emotional pain to chase their dream of competing at the highest level.

As an athlete you are *adaptable*. You are able to adjust on the fly and make corrections to plays or to your stroke in order to succeed in practice or in games. When something is not working during a game, you sense it and try to make adjustments in split seconds to make yourself better. A great example is a baseball pitcher who cannot throw his curveball for a strike. A coach may say, "Look, you don't have your best stuff today, but you are going to have to go out there and compete for a few innings; just give us a chance to win." The pitcher then tries to figure out a way to be successful to keep his team in the game. If you are a basketball player and your competition is faster than you, then you have to take different angles to get to where they are going to be faster. There are many other examples of having to adjust to your opponent; you can probably come up with your own example of being adaptable and making adjustments while competing.

The last quality to be mentioned is *focus*. Whatever you want to call it—"in the zone," "concentration," "runner's high," "dialed in," or something else—you are focused for a certain period of time. Many athletes have stated that this is the lure of athletic competition and what makes them keep coming back. There is no greater feeling than when things are "just clicking" or "working on all cylinders." There must be a game or event in which you competed when your mind was in such a good place that you experienced the euphoria of being a perfect athlete at that time. This is what athletes strive for time and time again. Even non-athletes strive for this kind of focus.

You may not have given much thought to all of these qualities, and you may exhibit many more besides these. Try to think about the qualities you have and how your sport has helped shape these traits. Even if you don't think so, "you got mad game" and don't forget it.

DUMB JOCK OR SUCCESSFUL DOC?

Everyone knows that stereotypes of student-athletes are alive and well. Many people don't know or don't think about all the transferable skills that athletes do possess, and because athletes are in the limelight so much, they become an easy target for folks who want to portray the negative side of athletics, like gambling and cheating. Fans, on the other hand, like to show up on Saturday and root for their team. Other people envy athletes and wish that they were more athletic themselves. Who hasn't dreamed of being a professional athlete some time in their life? You can add to the stereotypes or you can prove to your campus that you are an intelligent, dedicated student-athlete who will be successful in sport and in life. Here are a few examples of some very successful athletes (CNN Money, 2011, http://money.cnn.com/galleries/2011/news/companies/1104/gallery.fortune500_ceo_athletes.fortune/index.html; Sporting News, 2010, http://aol.sportingnews.com/mlb/feed/2010-09/smart-athletes/story/sporting-news-names-the-20-smartest-athletes-in-sports):

- Jeffrey Immelt is the Chief Executive Officer (CEO) of General Electric. He graduated from Dartmouth in 1978 and was a starting offensive tackle for the Big Green football team.
- Samuel J. Palmisano is the CEO of IBM. He never once missed practice as the center for the Johns Hopkins Blue Jays football team from 1970 through the 1972 seasons. His teams went 17–10 during his athletic career (Sporting News, 2010, http://aol.sportingnews.com/mlb/feed/2010-09/smart-athletes/story/sporting-news-names-the-20-smartest-athletes-in-sports).

- Myron Rolle is currently a safety with the Tennessee Titans. He was a Lott Trophy finalist and an Associated Press third team All-American. He graduated from Florida State in two and a half years with an Exercise Science degree and a 3.75 GPA. He received a master's in medical anthropology from Oxford and plans on being a neurosurgeon when his playing career is over.
- Pau Gasol is the starting forward for the Los Angeles Lakers. He left the University of Barcelona's medical school to pursue a professional basketball career and has won two NBA championships, was Rookie of the Year in 2002, and is a three-time All-Star.

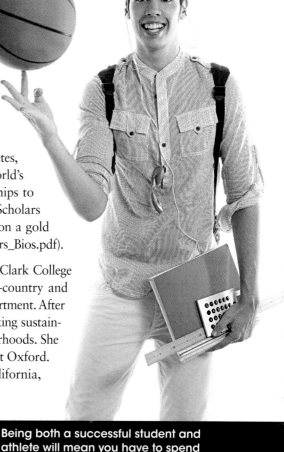

The 2011 Rhodes scholarship winners included several student-athletes, two of whom are profiled below. The Rhodes scholarship is one of the world's most renowned academic awards and winners are granted full scholarships to study at the University of Oxford in the United Kingdom. Former Rhodes Scholars include former President Clinton (1968) and Bill Bradley (1965), who won a gold medal in the Olympics (www.rhodesscholar.org/assets/uploads/2011_Winners_Bios.pdf).

- Tamma A. Carleton graduated summa cum laude from Lewis and Clark College in 2009, where she competed as a member of the Pioneers cross-country and track team. She worked as a research assistant in the economics department. After graduating she moved to Washington, D.C., and is interested in linking sustainable local agriculture to improved nutrition in low-income neighborhoods. She plans to do the M.Sc. in Environmental Change and Management at Oxford.
- Megan C. Braun graduated in October from the University of California, Irvine, where she was the goalie for the Anteaters water polo team. After graduation, she attended Cambridge University, where she studied the ethical constructs of war and peacemaking. Her senior thesis looked at the ways in which weapons technology desensitizes U.S. soldiers to loss of life. At Oxford, she plans to do the M.Phil. in International Relations. She is the University of California, Irvine's first Rhodes Scholar.

Being both a successful student and athlete will mean you have to spend time in both arenas.

Now, not all of you will go on to win Rhodes Scholarships, but how many of you have ever compared your sport to academics? Do you know how similar your sport is to the academic world? All you have to do is use your imagination to transfer the skills that you already have into each class you are "competing" in this term. After reviewing the table on the following page, try to make some more connections between your athletic life and your academic life.

ACTIVITY 1 Your Turn

Review the table on the following page, then think of some other similarities and enter them here:

_____

_____

_____

_____

_____

Athletics	Academics
Coach	**Professor**
1. Develops a practice plan each day	1. Lectures or teaches you about the course each time you meet
2. Prepares you for games	2. Gives you readings/assignments/homework to work on outside of class to prepare you for exams
3. Gives you feedback on your practice and technique	3. Grades your homework assignments and written work/provides feedback
4. Is in a position of authority/decides how much playing time you get	4. Is in a position of authority/Gives you your grade
5. Makes decisions on who gets cut from the team	5. Makes decision on what grade each student should receive
6. Is an expert in your sport	6. Is an expert in their field of study
Practice	**Class/Homework**
1. Practice on a consistent basis to get better	1. Attend class on a consistent basis to understand the material better
2. Work on your strengths and weaknesses at practice	2. Class is a place to ask questions about things you don't understand
3. Usually work at it until you get it right	3. Homework helps you master the subject area or understand it at a deeper level
4. Prepares you for games or competitions	4. Class/homework prepares you for exams/quizzes/papers
5. Once you've mastered something you work on something else	5. Spend more time on the homework you don't understand
6. Constantly practicing to get better at your sport and obtain a greater level of mastery	6. Can always continue to review your notes and homework to get better
Teammates	**Classmates**
1. People with a common interest	1. People in your class asked to master the same material
2. Work with your teammates to make the team better	2. Study groups work to make everyone better
3. Do drills together with teammates	3. Do group projects together with classmates
4. Ask each other questions to make sure you understand the play	4. Ask classmates for help or missed classwork
5. If you don't complete your assignment, the team can suffer	5. Group project must be completed together; one classmate's mistake can hurt the group
6. Sometimes work on practice in small groups with your teammates	6. Professors often ask students to work together in groups during or outside of class
7. You all study the same playbook	7. You all study the same books
Regular Season Games/Competitions	**Quizzes/Papers**
1. Chance to prove to your coach how good you are at your sport	1. Chance to prove to the professor how well you know the material
2. Evaluation of how you measure up against the competition	2. Evaluation of what grade will you get compared to the rest of the class (class may be graded on a curve)
3. Did you prepare properly for the game?	3. Are you ready for the quiz?/Did you put in enough effort on your paper?
4. Studied your opponent (game film)	4. Studied the material
5. Developed a game plan for each team	5. Developed a study plan
6. Know the other team's strengths and weaknesses (scouting report)	6. Know your strengths and weaknesses with the material
7. Worked with teammates to get ready	7. Studied with classmates to get ready
Postseason	**Midterms/Final Exams**
1. What you worked for all season	1. What you have learned the entire term
2. Why you worked so hard all season	2. The last test of your ability and knowledge of the course material
3. Better competition to face	3. Usually a tougher exam or longer paper
4. Culmination of all the work you have put into your sport	4. Culmination of all the work you have put in
5. More at stake	5. More at stake/bigger percentage of your grade
6. More pressure	6. More pressure/final exams usually longer

RESPECT THE OTHER PLAYERS

While you generally have respect for yourself, your teammates, your coaches, and other athletes on campus, sometimes athletes forget to respect and appreciate the talents of others. You may be able to run a hundred-yard dash in just over 10 seconds, but can you produce a movie, write a novel, paint an extraordinary picture, build an electric car, or carbon date a fossil? There are many talented people on your campus besides yourself. Think about the time and energy that these people must have put into their passion or craft. Though 65,000 fans may not show up to listen to a slam poetry reading, these poets are talented nonetheless and they deserve your respect. As you begin your journey through college or the university, don't forget to appreciate and show respect for others on your campus and off.

Individuals have different passions and talents—yours happens to be an athletic skill. It doesn't mean that your talent is better than others. Your university experience should be one of exploration, and what better way to explore than to attend events showcasing different talents on and around your campus? You don't have to like or be moved by all these events, but it will give you a greater appreciation of the different talents that individuals possess. It will also give you a greater appreciation for how hard others work.

Let's begin with your professors. Most professors have had to dedicate much of their life to going to school and passing exams. They have sacrificed many things to get to where they are, just like you. Most professors possess a master's and/or a doctoral degree. This means they have written many more papers than you, taken many more tests than you, and have conducted research in their area of interest for many years. They have dedicated themselves to academics for some time. You have a passion for your sport; they have a passion for their education and research. If you respect and appreciate the time they have dedicated to their specific subject area, they will most likely respect the time and energy that you have put into mastering your sport. Take the time to get to know them through office hours and try to understand what their passions are in their field of study.

When you go to inform them that you will be missing class for an athletic event, make sure you do not do this with a sense of entitlement. Do it with humility. They will help you succeed if you communicate with them appropriately and show respect for their time and efforts.

Here is an example of how to handle missed class time with your instructor during their office hours, not during class (SA = student-athlete, PN = Professor Nichols):

SA: Professor Nichols, my name is Jon Noxville and I am in your Psychology 201 class that meets on Tuesdays and Thursdays from 4:00 to 6:00 P.M.

PN: Yes, hello, Mr. Noxville. How may help you?

SA: I wanted to let you know that this class seems very interesting and I am dedicated to doing well, yet I am also a member of the men's soccer team here at WM University and I am going to be missing three days of class this quarter due to our soccer schedule. I hope that this is not a major issue because I would really like to do well in this class. Would it be OK if I turn

Good sportsmanship is a part of integrity.

my assignments in early when I am scheduled to travel with the team? I also noticed that there is a midterm scheduled for a day that I will be gone. Could I please take that exam early before we leave or after we get back, whichever is easiest for you? I understand that this may create a little more work for you, but I would appreciate any consideration on this.

PN: Do you have some sort of letter or can someone from the athletics department email me to verify these dates?

SA: Yes, my academic advisors (or coach) produce a letter like this. Would you like them to email it to you or can I bring it by class the next time we meet?

PN: Please bring it by the next time we meet. Once I have verification of your travel dates, I will make other arrangements for you. Can you make sure to continue to remind me as these dates get closer? You know that I only allow three unexcused absences and these will be your three?

SA: Yes, I understand and will attend class regularly. Thank you so much. I will remind you as the dates get closer. I know that this is an inconvenience for you, but I really appreciate it. Have a good day, Professor Nichols. See you in class.

In this scenario, you have addressed your professor appropriately, showed respect for their class, indicated that you take the class seriously, proven that you have read the syllabus, shown appreciation for their willingness to make alternative arrangements for you, and indicated that you will continue to communicate with them about your athletic obligations. Well done!

Here is the way it should *not* go down:

SA: Hey, professor, my name is Jon Noxville and I am on the soccer team here at WM University. I am going to be missing a few classes this quarter because I play soccer here.

PN: Do you know which dates you will be missing and do you have a letter from the athletics department verifying these dates?

SA: Yes.

PN: Can you provide me with such a letter, Mr. Noxville?

SA: Yes, and I think I am going to be missing a midterm too.

PN: Do you know the date?

SA: No, not right now.

PN: You did read the syllabus and understand that I only allow three excused absences?

SA: Oh, I think I am going to miss more than that.

PN: Will that be all, Mr. Noxville?

SA: I think so; later!

Obviously this is not a respectful exchange, but it happens regularly with athletes. This student-athlete needs a little practice with his communication skills. Keep reading and we will get there.

The first exchange is just one example of how to communicate and appreciate someone else on your campus. Think about others on your campus who put in countless hours practicing and mastering a different craft: Band members, dance/stunt team members, chess club members, advisors, tutors, chairs of departments, groundskeepers, and the like. All of these people have different talents and have worked hard to get to where they are.

YOU HAVE TO BE A GOOD RECRUITER TO GET TALENT THAT HELPS YOU WIN

Every great athletic program or sport has to have great recruiters. You cannot win without good talent and it takes time and energy to find that talent. Coaches spend much of their lives on the road recruiting the talent that they think will help their program be successful. This is your opportunity to be a "recruiter" for yourself. If you want to be academically successful, you have to find people that are going to help you achieve that goal.

In this section we will discuss what it means to be a good recruiter. After you have identified the talent, how do you get them to be a part of your team?

The first thing any good recruiter does is define what their team is going to be and what qualities they are looking for. Are they going to be fast and fly around the field, or are they going to just out muscle the other team and drive the ball down their throat? A track coach has to figure out in what events they can score their points. Is it in the distance events, sprints, jumps, or throws? A basketball coach has to decide if they are going to go with the bigs or go get some shooters from the outside. All these coaches/recruiters are establishing what they want their team identity to be—they are establishing goals.

Before you begin recruiting your own academic success team, you need to think about what your goals are: Do you what to earn your associate's degree, or be at the community college for one year and move on? Do you want to prepare yourself for graduate school or take care of your academics for three years so you can get drafted? These are the questions that need to be answered, but don't be surprised if your goals change along the way.

Coaches who are good recruiters watch and evaluate hundreds of athletes for just a few positions. They all have depth charts that rate a particular athlete's athletic ability, personal characteristics, family background, and academic profile to determine if they will be a good fit for the college/university and for the team. So you will need to get past some of your reservations and start meeting people who have potential talent for your academic success team. You are looking for people that can help you be successful and help you achieve your academic goals. Believe it or not, once you start looking, this talent is not hard to find. Colleges and universities are full of people that want to help you succeed.

Look for people who are going to be honest with you and hold you accountable. Too many star athletes surround themselves with "yes people"; all they say is yes. Think about the recent story regarding the New Orleans Saints "bounty" scandal, in which defensive players were allegedly offered bonuses for causing injury or harm to opposing players. It seems that no one was willing to step forward and say no. Athletics departments are always trying to protect their image. There is nothing wrong with this, as long as they are being honest with themselves and protecting a true image. When you are a "big time" college athlete, many people tell you what you want to hear: "You are great, you are going to make millions, you make this university so much money, and you can write your own ticket from here." Do you get better at your sport when your coaches are just saying "You're great; you don't need to work on anything"? Absolutely not, so don't allow yourself to be surrounded by people who are

Use your teamwork skills to help you be successful in college.

not going to be honest with you, hold you accountable, and strive to make you better. If you decide that you are not going to go to class, who is going to give you a little kick in the backside and say "Get your fanny out of bed and get to class, you're not good enough yet at algebra to slack off"? This is who you want on your team. Just like you would want a coach to tell you how to get better, tell you when you make mistakes, and raise their expectations for you, you want the same thing from your academic success team.

Don't allow others to do your work for you. Do you let other people on your team play for you? No! This would be insulting to an athlete and it is insulting to your academic ability as well. This is not just referring to homework or papers. This means making your own phone calls to make appointments and registering for your own classes, which begins with looking up classes that count toward your degree, are interesting to you, and have value to you. Walk your own forms to the records office. Set up your own advising appointments. You have to think about how you want to be remembered and how people will perceive you. What do you want your legacy to be? Do you want to be the athlete that couldn't do anything for themselves or the exceptional athlete that takes care of their business on and off the field? You are too good to let others do the work for you. Rise to the challenge and don't be afraid to find out what you may be capable of academically.

Let's talk about where your recruiting pool is going to come from. First and foremost, do you have family that will hold you accountable? If so, then you need to communicate with them on a regular basis about how you are doing academically. Don't get confused here; your mom or dad should not be calling the athletics department and telling the athletic director that you are struggling in Biology 101. This means a parent who will say to you, "If you are struggling, then you need to find out who can help you. Are there tutors available to you? Have you talked with your professor? Have you notified your coach and athletics advisor?" And then they will follow up with you and say, "Did you get that taken care of?"

Let's consider your friends next. Are your friends good study partners? Are they people who will wake you up when you have class or practice that morning? Or are they people you just want to party with? If they are just people you party with, don't put them on your team. They are probably a lot of fun, but at a certain point you have to get your work done. Try to surround yourself with people who know what your academic goals are and have similar or higher goals than you. As an athlete you want people to push you, because until you are pushed, you don't know what you are capable of. This can be uncomfortable, but the reward is spectacular. Choose these friends wisely.

You may want to include an academic advisor (or several) on your team. Some athletics departments even have their own athletics advisors. These can be people who help you identify your academic goals, help you take ownership of your education, refer you to appropriate resources, and provide academic support. There are other advisors on campus as well. Find one or more that take a genuine interest in your success; these are the ones you want on your team.

Professors can be a part of your team as well. Most professors teach because they love educating young people and have a genuine passion for seeing students learn. There are others who have tenure and are just riding the gravy train to retirement. Don't invite the gravy train riders to be on your team. Remember that you are only as good as your weakest link. Don't have weak links. Find professors that can relate to you, want to see you be successful, support your efforts on and off the field, push you to learn more than you thought you could, and hold you accountable for getting the work done.

Coaches can be on your team as well. Here is a chance for you to recruit them. Make sure they take an interest in your success outside of athletic competition. Do they ask you questions about how you are doing in school? Can you go to them if you are struggling academically? If the answer to these questions is "no," then don't include

STUDENT PROFILE

Jamal is a first-year student-athlete and didn't have many reservations coming to a highly competitive four-year university. He grew up doing most things on his own. He took the city bus to and from school, completed most of his homework with no help before basketball practice, fixed his own dinner when he got home, and even prepared his younger brother and sister for school each morning. Confident and mature, he didn't think he needed any help when he got to college. Besides, "high school wasn't that hard" and he had received a 3.00 cumulative high school grade point average by studying after school and before practice.

He knew he was a good basketball player and thought he would be OK his first year at school because "everything had worked out so far with a scholarship and admission to a great school." But his new practice schedule was tough and he was always exhausted at the end of each day. "I just wanted to go to bed because I knew I had to be back up at 6:00 A.M. each morning for weightlifting."

"I got a little concerned about my academics when I felt like everyone in my class understood all the material and I didn't." He later found out that the average GPA of all students who were admitted to his university was 3.91 and had completed on average 21 units of college credits before they arrived, either by taking Advanced Placement exams or by completing courses through community colleges during high school. Jamal had no college credits coming in. He began to feel as if he did not belong. He was having a hard time making friends outside of the basketball team and some of the older members of the team knew he was competing to take their starting position. Jamal wasn't used to reaching out and asking for help.

His coaches had told him during the recruiting process that this was a highly academic institution and that earning a degree from the university carried a lot of weight amongst employers across the country. Jamal quickly fell behind in his courses and didn't want to let anyone know because he felt ashamed and overwhelmed. He

failed two midterms and received a low C on another one. He knew he wasn't doing well, but felt embarrassed to let people know.

"It was about halfway through the term before I really decided to ask for some help." He didn't have much practice asking for help, but he went to his athletics academic advisor and explained what was going on. The advisor quickly assigned him some tutors and helped Jamal devise a study/time management plan. "The advisor spent so much time with me helping me devise a plan; I just wish I had gone in there earlier."

"I felt like I wasn't going to be able to cut it at this school because everyone was *so* smart and I had only gotten in through athletics." Jamal met with his tutors regularly and began to realize that he could understand the material with a little extra effort. "I was still exhausted from school, athletics, and everything else, but with a good schedule I realized I could do the work." He talked to his instructors whose midterms he had failed and they encouraged him to come to their office hours and ask questions if he had them on a regular basis. "The tutors, the time management schedule, and working with my instructors really helped. Everyone was so nice and wanted to help me." Once Jamal received a few good grades on his quizzes and a couple papers he realized that he could compete in the classroom with everyone else. "I just needed a little confidence and to do well on a couple of assignments to feel like I belonged, it was like getting a couple open looks on the court and draining them. Just a little confidence gave me a great boost."

This is a common occurrence with college students. They do not utilize the resources or the people that are there to help, either out of fear or a lack of knowing where to go on campus. Have the courage to ask for help, because there is a great team on your campus just waiting to hear from you and they have the knowledge and skills to help you be successful. Push your reservations aside and don't be afraid to utilize a team of individuals on your campus to help you be successful.

them on your team. They just got cut from your team. If they are someone you can trust, then put them in the lineup.

There are probably others on campus you can include on your team, but you get the idea. Once you have built your team, now what? These are the people you ask questions of, tell when you are struggling, ask for help from, call when you do well, and invite to your graduation. There are going to be times when you struggle academically, emotionally, socially, or just need someone to talk to. These are the people that will listen and help you get through it. You need to also understand what the strengths are of each of your team members. A friend may be a good person to talk to when you have problems with a boyfriend or girlfriend. Your coach may be good for when you have difficulties with a teammate or another coach. A professor could be a good resource for career advising or helping you with ideas for a paper in another class. Your advisor may be able to refer you to the right resources on campus for financial aid or to set up free tutoring. You have to be able to identify their strengths and weaknesses; this is how you decide who to go to when the game is on the line. You recruited them, so put some trust in them and let them know that they are valued. A simple "thank you" goes a long way with people on your team.

YOU MEAN I HAVE TO DO THAT, TOO?

Every student-athlete hears from their coach that they have additional responsibilities that other students don't have, but what does this really mean? This section will begin with some very simple additional responsibilities and end with what athletics really means to a college or university campus.

Let's start with the extra time commitments that you have: As an athlete you are expected/required (depending on who you talk to) to practice on a regular basis. When most people think of practice they think of the two to four hours of work you do specific to your sport. For example, if you are a baseball player, it is the time you spend at batting practice and fielding ground balls. If you are a tennis player, it is the time you spend on the courts hitting with your teammates and coach. If you are a volleyball player, it may the time you spend preparing for the other team's designed plays. This is indeed practice, but as athletes you know that this is just the tip of the iceberg of your time commitment. Not everyone on your campus realizes that in addition to the sport-specific practice you do, you are in the weight room for an hour or two each day before or after practice; in the coaches' offices or in a film room breaking down film of yourself, your team, and the other team for hours a week preparing for practice and games; attending clinics and camps in the off season; doing community service each term; traveling to and from competitions and tournaments; doing off-season conditioning with a trainer; rehabbing injuries; and attending "voluntary workouts" or "captain's camps." (Coaches and compliance officers call them "voluntary"; athletes on the team call them "mandatory." If anyone thinks these are voluntary, just don't show up and see what happens to your chances of making the team the next season.)

At the NCAA level teams are limited to 20 hours per week of practice and must have one mandatory day off. However, most student-athletes know that these hours only include the time on the field, in the pool, or on the courts—coaches know how to get more hours in during the week. It does not include weights, "voluntary" workouts, conditioning, and everything else outside of practice.

You may be thinking, "Yeah, you're right, I do put in a lot of time! This school should understand that and treat me a little better!" But remember, *you chose to be a student-athlete.* No one forced this choice on you, so don't expect people to feel sorry for you because you work so hard. You are not an entitled athlete—you are a privileged one.

Because of these extra time commitments, it is essential that you manage your time wisely. Keep reading; the time management section is coming up soon. Before

Sometimes college and sports is a juggling act.

you get there you need to understand that you have other responsibilities outside of your sport.

Most student-athletes have extra academic responsibilities that they must follow to remain eligible. For instance, at the NCAA Division I level all student-athletes must have 40% of their degree completed by the end of their second year (www.ncaa.org). They must pass a minimum of 6 "degree applicable" units each term (in the sport of football it is now 9 semester or 8 quarter degree applicable units during the fall term to be eligible the following fall (NCAA Bylaw 14.4). If you are competing at a community college, an NAIA school (www.naia.org), NCAA Division II or III, or any other regionally or nationally governed athletics association, you most likely have some academic rules you must comply with to be eligible. Make sure you understand these rules so that you do not render yourself ineligible. Someone on your academic success team may be able to help you. Here are some websites that may also be helpful:

California Community College Commission on Athletics (COA): www.cccaasports.org

Eastern College Athletic Conference (ECAC): www.ecac.org

National Association of Intercollegiate Athletics (NAIA): www.naia.org

National Christian College Athletic Association (NCCAA): www.thenccaa.org

National Collegiate Athletic Association (NCAA): www.ncaa.org

National Junior College Athletic Association (NJCAA): www.njcaa.org

United States Collegiate Athletic Association (USCAA): www.theuscaa.com

Another responsibility you undertake is that you are easily identifiable on your campus. You may feel targeted at times because you are an athlete, but it is your reality and you must deal with it responsibly. Remember, you made this choice to be a student-athlete.

Society wants to read and hear about controversy. You don't see John White or Stacy Black's name on the front page of your local newspaper if they decide to trade lab beakers for some "skin ink" at a local tattoo parlor. However, if you were the starting quarterback for the Ohio State Buckeyes and you traded some of your athletics department–issued gear for tattoos, you would be declared ineligible, your multimillion-dollar-a-year coach could be forced to resign, your athletic director would be told his department lacks institutional control and humiliated on public television, and the president of the university would be blasted in the newspapers, ESPN, the radio, blogs, and websites. One website dedicated only to bringing society the dirt on athletes is badjocks.com Ohio State made the website not too long ago.

There are people who profit from student-athlete controversy. They will sling your name in the mud and even make stories up because you are a celebrity when you are a student-athlete and society loves to read and hear about celebrity controversies.

You can be targeted even on your own campus because you are so identifiable. You often wear your gear to class ; you travel and miss class; you sometimes show up late or not at all because you are worn out from practice or you just don't want to go; your names are in the papers; when you have projects, papers to write, or speeches to give you usually talk about athletics because you are passionate and knowledgeable about it. This is all fine, but you need to realize that you are easy to pick out of a crowd.

Some negative things have been mentioned, but you also need to remember that you have been put in a position to make some real positive impacts, both on and off campus. When you go to elementary schools to play with local youth, it can be the highlight of their day. When you score the winning basket with no time left on the clock, thousands of people are in a state of utter joy for you and their team. When your academic advisor gets a phone call from one of your professors and says "That student-athlete was so on the ball and communicated with me so well throughout the quarter; I wish all students would communicate that way," it makes them reaffirm why they chose to go into that profession of helping young people. There are so many good things that can come from being a student-athlete: money, self-worth, discipline, a good work ethic, competitiveness, a commitment to succeed, and many others.

Here comes the "granddaddy" benefit: Hardly anyone ever tells you this, or you don't understand it, but you represent the entire college or university you attend. How many students on your campus travel all around the state and nation (sometimes the world) with the name of your school across their chest, back, or on their head? The answer is not many. Baseball teams play an excess of 60 games a year and usually half of them are on the road. When you travel to these places you stay in hotels, interact with people in the community, go to their restaurants, and compete in front of their fans. At larger universities you are even on television and radio across the country. Notre Dame football is playing a game in Ireland in 2012.

The question that needs to be answered is, how do you want yourself and your institution to be perceived in your community and in all the communities you travel to throughout your athletic career?

ACTIVITY 2 Identify the Differences

Jot down eight ways that you feel student-athletes get treated differently than regular students on or off campus.

Get together with a partner and think of eight responsibilities that other students may have that you don't (e.g., other students may have to work full time). Discuss with your partner the similarities and differences between student-athletes and non-student-athletes.

STRENGTH AND BALANCE

Strengthen your core academic skills so that you can balance all that you have to do.

The last section discussed your extra responsibilities, which included time commitments. This section will help you develop an effective technique to deal with these commitments. The first thing you have to do is determine what kind of student you want to be, what kind of athlete you want to be, and how important your social life is. Once you have these goals laid out for yourself, then you can begin to lay out a time management plan for each area of your life: athletic, academic, and social.

The most important thing you should remember is be proactive instead of reactive. When you are proactive you set deadlines for yourself and plan ahead. For instance, if you have an eight-page research paper due in two weeks you can devise a plan to write one page every night for eight days, take it in to your tutor or writing lab on the tenth day, make revisions on the eleventh day, and turn it when it is due. This would be a proactive approach to your paper.

A reactive approach would be waiting until the last day and then trying to throw together an eight-page paper the night before it is due. Everyone knows the proactive approach is much better, but students still procrastinate on these things. Being proactive takes work and you have to commit to it during each term, just like practicing every day for your sport. You didn't get good because you just showed up on game days. You have put in a lot of work to get where you are and school assignments can be accomplished with the same approach. Here are some other examples of proactive and reactive behaviors:

Proactive	Reactive
Sign up for tutors early	Wait until you receive a D on your first midterm to ask for a tutor
Inform your professor that you will be missing class and would like to turn in your homework early on the days you will miss	Tell your professor you will be missing class tomorrow and ask if you can turn in your homework when you get back from your trip
Let your advisor know that you are struggling in a course as soon as you know the course is challenging	Tell your advisor at the end of the term that you don't think you did well in a specific course and were wondering if it will affect your eligibility
Plan out a course schedule prior to your enrollment time	Call your advisor the day you register and tell them you don't know which courses to register for
Schedule a meeting with a financial advisor the first week of each term to go over your financial aid agreement	Call a financial aid advisor after your courses are dropped because you didn't pay your fees
Schedule an appointment with a career advisor two times per year	Try to get an appointment with a career advisor two weeks before you graduate because you are applying for jobs and need a resume

This is not rocket science; you simply need to develop a proactive plan and stick to it. Evaluate yourself at the end of each day to see how much you accomplished. Reward yourself when you achieve your goals. If you are a movie buff, go to the movies. If you like video games, then buy yourself a new video game. Do not allow yourself to continually put things off until the last minute. This approach may have worked in high school, but it will not work consistently in college. Getting good grades takes consistent, hard work, just like your sport.

ACTIVITY 3 Plan Your Time

Pull out a syllabus for one of your courses and fill out the spreadsheet in Exhibit 1 on the following page. Complete the spreadsheet by writing in which week and day assignments, homework, and papers are due. There is also a completed example for you to look at (Exhibit 2).

EXHIBIT **1** Term Schedule for _____

	SUN	MON	TUE	WED	THU	FRI	SAT
WEEK 1							
WEEK 2							
WEEK 3							
WEEK 4							
WEEK 5							
WEEK 6							
WEEK 7							
WEEK 8							
WEEK 9							
WEEK 10							
WEEK 11							
WEEK 12							
WEEK 13							
WEEK 14							
WEEK 15							
WEEK 16							
FINALS							

EXHIBIT **2** Term Schedule for _____

	SUN	MON	TUE	WED	THU	FRI	SAT
WEEK 1							
WEEK 2				Game	Math quiz 1	Travel day	Game
WEEK 3			COMS group pre-sentation 1		Math quiz 2	Travel day	Game
WEEK 4		Psych exam 1		Math exam 1/Game			Game
WEEK 5			COMS speech 1	Travel to away game	Math quiz 3		Game
WEEK 6		Psych paper 1 due		Game	COMS exam 1	Travel day	Game

	SUN	MON	TUE	WED	THU	FRI	SAT
WEEK 7					Math quiz 4		Game
WEEK 8			COMS group pre-sentation 2	Travel to away game	COMS paper 1 due		Game
WEEK 9		Psych exam 2		Math exam 2		Parents coming to town	Game
WEEK 10			COMS speech 2	Game	COMS exam 2/ Math quiz 5	Travel day	Game
WEEK 11				Psych paper 2 due			Game
WEEK 12		Psych exam 3		Travel to away game	Math quiz 6		
WEEK 13				Math exam 3	COMS exam 3		Team banquet
WEEK 14			COMS speech 3		COMS paper 2 due		
WEEK 15			COMS group pre-sentation 3		Math quiz 7		
WEEK 16							
FINALS			Psych final 10:00 A.M.		Math final exam 2:00 P.M.	COMS final exam 7:00 A.M.	

Next, think about what your days include (practice, class, homework/studying, sleeping, eating, and fun time for yourself) and fill out a weekly schedule (Exhibit 3). An example of an athletic schedule for a week is provided in Exhibit 4.

EXHIBIT 3 Student-Athlete Time Management Worksheet Week of ____/____

TIME	SUN	MON	TUE	WED	THU	FRI	SAT
6:00 A.M.							
6:30							
7:00							
7:30							
8:00							

TIME	SUN	MON	TUE	WED	THU	FRI	SAT
8:30							
9:00							
9:30							
10:00							
10:30							
11:00							
11:30							
NOON							
12:30 P.M.							
1:00							
1:30							
2:00							
2:30							
3:00							
3:30							
4:00							
4:30							
5:00							
5:30							
6:00							
6:30							
7:00							
7:30							
8:00							
8:30							
9:00							
9:30							
10:00							
10:30							
11:00							
11:30							
Midnight							
12:30							
1-6 A.M.							

EXHIBIT **4** **Student-Athlete Time Management Worksheet Week of ____/____**

TIME	SUN	MON	TUE	WED	THU	FRI	SAT
6:00 A.M.							
6:30			Wake up		Wake up		
7:00		Wake up	Weights	Wake up	Weights		
7:30		Breakfast	Weights	Breakfast	Weights		
8:00		ENG 134	Weights	Engl 134	Weights		
8:30			Weights		Weights		Wake up
9:00			Breakfast		Breakfast	Wake up	Breakfast
9:30						Breakfast	
10:00		Bus 214	Bio office hours (if needed)	Bus 214	Bio office hours (if needed)	Bus 214	Practice
10:30	Wake up						Practice
11:00	Breakfast	Bus 214	Lunch	Bio	Lunch	Study Hall	Practice
11:30	Study	Tutor		Tutor		Study Hall	Practice
NOON	Study	Lunch	Bio 115	Lunch	Bio 115	Lunch	Practice
12:30 P.M.	Study						Lunch
1:00	Study	Study Hall		Study Hall		Study Hall	
1:30	Lunch	Study Hall		Study Hall		Study Hall	
2:00		Practice	Practice	Practice	Practice	Practice	
2:30	Study	Practice	Practice	Practice	Practice	Practice	
3:00	Study	Practice	Practice	Practice	Practice	Practice	
3:30	Study	Practice	Practice	Practice	Practice	Practice	
4:00	Study	Practice	Practice	Practice	Practice	Practice	
4:30					Relax!!!		
5:00			Meeting w/ Coordinator				
5:30							
6:00	Dinner	Dinner	Dinner	Dinner	Dinner	Dinner	Dinner
6:30							
7:00		Study Hall	Bio 115 Lab	Study Hall	Relax!!!		
7:30		Study Hall		Study Hall			
8:00		Study Hall		Study Hall			
8:30		Study Hall		Study Hall			

TIME	SUN	MON	TUE	WED	THU	FRI	SAT
9:00							
9:30							
10:00		Sleep	Sleep	Sleep	Sleep	Sleep	
10:30							
11:00							
11:30							
Midnight							
12:30							
1–6 A.M.							

Use a calendar on your phone to hold yourself accountable and to create a list of things to do each day and cross them off as you complete them. There are great apps for this available on many smartphones.

ONLY TALK TRASH WHEN IT'S APPROPRIATE

Let's begin this section with a word about cell phones. Your cell is most likely your primary form of communication. You can check your email, send text messages, download apps, tweet, and talk on it. You can do many other things on it as well, but don't do those things while you are in class, at practice, meeting with your professor, or meeting with anyone else who is a staff member on campus (academic advisor, financial aid officer, admissions representative, etc.). Most likely you are meeting with these people because you have some questions that you would like to have answered. Don't take up somebody's time and then begin texting in their office. They will not appreciate it and they will remember you for it—and not in a good way. You want to leave a good impression, especially on those who are now on your academic success team. Turn the cell on vibrate or silent and return phone calls and texts on your own time. Does your coach allow you to have your cell phone on during a practice? Treat your professors and other university/college staff like you would treat your coach.

OK, let's move on. You cannot communicate with everyone on campus the same way. You might speak to your coach a certain way, but that may not work with your professor. You can probably get away with being much more casual with your coach or assistant coach. When you get to know your professors better, addressing them in a casual manner may be all right, but for now be safe and address them appropriately. What does this mean? It means when you address them in person call them Doctor or Professor, not Dave. When you introduce yourself to them, indicate which class you are enrolled in. Professors teach a lot of students, so they probably will not know who you are the first couple times you speak with them.

When you email them, make sure it comes from an appropriate email account. To be safe, it is always encouraged to use your school email address when communicating with people on campus and your personal address when you are communicating in a less formal setting. Your school email address identifies you as a student at your school and many professors, with FERPA (Family Educational Rights and Privacy Act) laws, will not respond to emails coming from personal accounts such as Hotmail, Yahoo, Gmail, and the like. Also, you should know that when security issues arise with Yahoo, Gmail, and other email providers your campus IT department may not allow those emails to get transmitted to campus email addresses. For example, if a hacker was able to obtain personal information on Yahoo subscribers, your campus will probably not allow emails to go through from Yahoo accounts. "No big deal," you may say. But what if you tried to email in a 10-page paper that was due and you find out later that your professor never received the paper? Not only this, but it clearly states in the syllabus that your professor will not accept late assignments. You may say "This was not my fault," but the reality is that it *is* your fault that your professor did not receive your paper on time. Ever get called for a bad foul in your sport? You can only argue for so long and the referee doesn't usually change their call, right? It is the same thing with regards to your classes—don't expect professors to change the rules for you.

Use correct grammar and punctuation when communicating with staff members on campus. Many students capitalize everything or don't capitalize anything when emailing their friends, tweeting, or communicating on Facebook. Do not fall into this habit when dealing with college/university staff. Below is a sample email for you to read:

> Professor Margera,
>
> My name is Rhianne Dunn (student ID #887665432). I am in Art 101 that meets Mondays and Wednesdays 4:00–6:00 P.M.. I am not feeling well. The health center prescribed antibiotics, which I will be taking for the next couple days, so I will be unable to attend class tomorrow. I have arranged to get the notes for the scheduled Monet discussion from a classmate. If I have questions, I plan to come by during your office hours. For anything not on the syllabus, please feel free to email me back.
>
> Thank you,
> Rhianne

Channel your aggression appropriately and use it to motivate you to do better.

The strong points of this email are:

1. It addresses the instructor appropriately.
2. It indicates which class the student is in and the day and time it meets.
3. It tells the instructor why the student cannot attend class and it gives advance notice; it is not written 10 minutes before class begins.
4. It indicates to the instructor that the student has read the syllabus and knows what is happening in class.
5. It indicates to the instructor that the student will be proactive about getting the class notes and seeking out the professor if there are questions.
6. It ends with "thank you."

If you have a separate athletic advisor, you can probably have more casual interactions with them because you get to know them better. Make sure you are aware that you cannot always communicate with your major advisors the same way you communicate with your athletic advisors. Athletics advisors usually understand what you go through on a daily basis and understand when you say "I am so tired today because coach got mad at our practice and made us do 'suicides' until four of us puked." You can't say this to your major advisor. They don't know what a "suicide" is in sports and they do not want to hear about your teammates vomiting. There may be exceptions, but tread lightly at first, especially if they are someone you are recruiting to be on your academic success team. Call them Mr. or Ms. to be polite. When in doubt, just ask people how they would like to be addressed.

When you make appointments with people on campus, keep those appointments and show up on time. Use a planner or calendar in your smartphone to remember these dates and times. Time has been set aside for you to meet with someone and many times they have spent time preparing for you and your meeting. They have pulled your degree audit, looked up your financial aid agreement, or maybe looked up your admissions application file. Be respectful of their time and get to their office a few minutes early. If you are going to see an advisor, bring your "curriculum sheet" or a copy of your degree audit with you. If you are going to see a professor, make sure you have spent some time clearly articulating what your questions are and what answers you would like to get. Several students are usually waiting in line to see professors during office hours. Some meetings you cannot prepare for, but if you can prepare in advance, make sure you do. People will remember you because you are identifiable, and if you show up prepared they will be happy to meet with you again. They may even walk down the hall to their colleagues and say, "I just had one of our women's basketball players in my office and that young woman was so prepared. I was impressed." You just earned some "brownie" points with someone on your campus—well done!

Tutors are another group you may have interactions with. They may be undergraduate students, graduate students, current athletes, or people from the community who want to help you be successful. If you have scheduled tutor meetings, then show up prepared. Tutors are not hired to do the work for you; they meet with you to help clarify material and help you with study habits. They are not going to be sitting next to you during midterms and final exams, so don't rely on them to do too much. If you are supposed to have read Chapters 5 to 7 before your tutoring session, then read them and write down questions that you have regarding the reading. If you meet with your tutor to go over math homework, then do the homework beforehand and mark where you have questions. This is the best way to utilize tutoring. Make sure your tutors understand how you learn best as well. If you need to see how problems are done on a board, then you and your tutor should schedule meetings in a room that has a whiteboard.

With regards to communication, find out from your tutor during your first meeting the best way to contact them. Is it calling, texting, or emailing? Give them advance notice if you cannot make a session. If you are unable to attend a session, let your coach and advisor know as well. Many times, tutors are required to submit evaluations after each tutoring session and you do not want your coach to find out from someone other than yourself that you were not there. Keep everyone in the loop so that there are no surprises. If you find that a tutor is not as helpful as you may have thought, let someone on your academic success team know, so that you can meet with a different tutor or find some extra help. If you make this communication a priority, you will build trust with people.

Finally we will address communication through the social media. You already know that you are in the spotlight, so don't add fuel to the fire by posting inappropriate material on your Twitter or Facebook account. Whether you are at the University of Alabama or Cerro Coso Community College, there are individuals who look for controversial material to blog about or post on another website. Athletes are an easy target and if you post things that put a big target on your back, sooner or later you will get struck.

Restrict who can view your pages and monitor who is following you on Twitter and Facebook. One hundred and forty characters just got Voula Papachristou, from Greece, banned from her first appearance at the 2012 Olympic Games. The headline read "Hot Greek Olympian Booted from Games over Racist Tweet" (www.badjocks.com, July 25, 2012). This is not the way most athletes would like to be remembered. You will be out and about in the community interacting with boosters and young children. Many of these kids know how to use the social media better than you do. You do not need little Chrissy Pontius from Dunn Elementary School going home and telling her parents that an athlete she met at school tweeted some nasty words about the opposing team. Simply ask yourself when tweeting or posting on Facebook: "Would I want my parents to see or read this"? If the answer is no, then don't post it.

Don't post when you are angry, sad, or just emotional in general. As a rule of thumb, don't post after midnight; nothing good usually happens after midnight. Get a good night's rest, gain some clarity, and then post if you like.

HE SHOOTS, HE SCORES, GOOOOOOOOOOOOAAAAAAAAAAAAAAL!

First, let's agree that a goal is something that you want to achieve. Goals can include athletic goals, academic goals, and personal goals, or whatever other goals you would like to accomplish. Here are some examples of some goals:

Athletic: I would like to be the starting striker for the women's soccer team by the beginning of my sophomore year.

Academic: I would like to achieve B's on all my midterms; however, I will be happy with a C in statistics.

Personal: I would like to find a place to live next year that I can afford and live with room-mates I get along with.

Spiritual: I would like to find a church that I am comfortable with by the end of the first term and attend at least once a month.

In these examples you can see that some of these goals are short term; for example, "achieving B's on all my midterms." Some of them are for longer period of time; for example, "being the starting striker by my sophomore year." You have to have some sort of timeframe on your goals that hold you accountable. If you are familiar with the acronym SMAC, you know that your goals need to be Specific, Measurable, Achievable, and Challenging. The only addition may be to add a timeframe within which to achieve these goals. For easy reference, a short-term goal can be considered anything within a month. Anything beyond a month can be considered a long-term goal. If a month feels like a short-term goal to you, then go ahead and create your own timeframe.

Athletes set goals for themselves all the time. Sometimes your sport just takes care of this itself. In track and field, athletes are always setting personal records ("PR'ing") during practice or at meets. Track athletes are constantly trying to "PR" in their specific event. Baseball players are usually trying to hit over 300, have a fielding percentage above 980, or have a strikeout-to-walk ratio of at least 3:1. These are goals that athletes strive for all the time. Reflecting back to "You Already Got Mad Game," you just need to transfer those skills.

Setting athletic, academic, and personal goals are important, and as an athlete you should be doing this on a regular basis. It is amazing what you can achieve and how much easier you can make your life if you hold yourself accountable for achieving certain goals by a certain time. Here are few exercises for you to try.

ACTIVITY 4   Set Your Goal

Pick one class that you are enrolled in right now and set a specific goal of what grade you would like to receive on your next assignment.

Specific Goal: _____

What are the steps you are going to take to reach this goal?

1.

2.

3.

What are the obstacles that may prevent you from achieving this goal?

1.

2.

3.

How can you combat these obstacles?

1.

2.

3.

Who can help hold you accountable for achieving this goal?

1.

2.

3.

Now repeat the exercise above, but for a specific athletic goal and personal goal.

Goals are not hard to set—they are hard to stay committed to. Luckily, athletes know how to stay committed. After your winter break, around the beginning of January, watch how many ads there are and how many stores are selling fitness equipment. Why? It is because the number one New Year's resolution is to lose weight or get in better shape (www.goalsguy.com). The problem is most people don't commit to it for longer than a couple of months and then they have a garage full of fitness equipment that collects dust. This equipment usually gets sold on Craigslist or at a garage sale a couple of months after purchase. As an athlete you know that two months is nothing if you want to be good at something. Nobody practices for two months and is a master of their sport.

When setting goals you have to develop a system that will hold you accountable on a regular basis. Some student-athletes like to write things down in a planner; others like to type them into their phone; and still others will use a personal calendar. It does not matter what method you use as long as you don't give up or forget your goals. An example is shown in Exhibit 5.

EXHIBIT 5 **Weekly Objectives**

Name:

Semester/Year: **Week of:**

Email:

Class	Objectives	Obj. Met
Bio 101	Read Chapters 1 and 2 and make notes	
	Complete online quiz by Wed @ 6 P.M.	
	Rewrite notes after class, but before practice	

Class	Objectives	Obj. Met
Soc 100	Create thesis and outline for paper due next week	
	Read Chapters 3 and 4	
	Talk to professor about travel and game in 2 wks	

Class	Objectives	Obj. Met
Mus 110	Download and listen to required music by tomorrow	
	Set up initial meeting with group by Tues	
	Go to professor's office hours and ask the ?	

Class	Objectives	Obj. Met
Non-clas-related	See advisor about upcoming registration	
	Talk to coach about practice times for next term	
	Complete required financial aid agreement	
	Buy Mother's Day card by end of the week	

Class	Objectives	Obj. Met

The last thing you need to remember when it comes to goals is to reward yourself when you achieve your goals. In sports that reward is usually intrinsic. Your coach gives you a pat on the back or your teammate gives you a slap on the bottom. You have to get in the habit of telling yourself how well you did when you achieve your own goals, both athletic and academic. Make sure your goals are Specific, Measurable, Achievable, and Challenging (and if you would like, put a timetable on it). As an athlete you already know how to do this; just transfer the skill to another area of your life and you will see the rewards immediately. You will also find that by completing your goals in timely fashion you will have much more free time for yourself.

BIG FISH, SMALL POND

You have probably always been the best or close to the best athlete on your team. You probably excelled when you were little and all the way through high school. Through your sport, you have gained confidence and the respect of others. Now that you are in college it can be a new ballgame, because just about everyone else on your team was the best athlete on their high school team as well. If you know this going in, then you will be better prepared. This can be a shock to many athletes and some have a hard time dealing with the fact that they are not the best anymore. Some athletes will blame their coach for not seeing their ability and just playing the returners. Some athletes may blame their new training regimen. It could be the strength and conditioning coach's fault or the trainer's fault. The reality is that you have to take ownership of your own effort. There are many things you have no control over, but you do control your own attitude and effort.

If you find yourself struggling with your confidence or starting to blame others for your lack of playing time or your injuries, then you probably just need a "gut check." Remind yourself that you know how to work hard and that this is under your control. If you find that

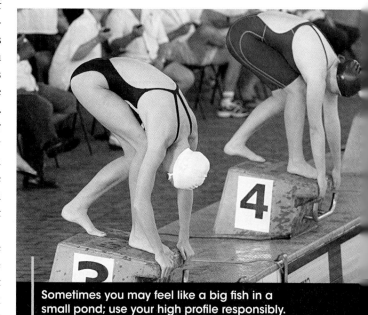

Sometimes you may feel like a big fish in a small pond; use your high profile responsibly.

your emotions are getting away from you and you are feeling depression or a lot of anxiety, make sure that you let somebody on your success team know what is going on. Be proactive and get some help before it spirals out of control. Talk to your coach about your training or ask them in a professional manner why you are not playing as much as you think you should. There is nothing wrong with this approach.

Your coach wants the best team or individuals out on the playing field that give him or her the best opportunity to win. One big mistake you don't want to make is letting your parents or guardians ask a coach these questions. For most coaches, their sport is a full-time job and they take a lot of pride in their work. Do not insult them by having your parents call or email on your behalf. There is absolutely nothing wrong with asking a coach for their evaluation of you. As long as they are honest, then you know where you stand and why.

Maybe you had a much different practice plan in high school or maybe you are feeling misled from the time you got recruited. Communicate with your coach in a one-on-one setting about your frustrations and questions. If you are feeling intimidated by your coach, talk to someone on your academic success team about what approach to take. Remember, you may need to communicate with your coach differently than you do with your advisor or professors. Express your concerns to someone you trust and ask them how you can approach your coach about the situation. Have the confidence to approach them in a professional manner. If they do not reciprocate the respect you showed them, then maybe this is a sign that you need to find somewhere else to compete. Not all coaches are the best fit for every athlete. Some athletes want their coaches to be "all up in their face" and push them, whereas other athletes may appreciate a calmer approach. This is your experience, so you have some choice in who you decide to play for.

If you felt misled on your recruiting trip, then let the coach know this. Most coaches do not promise starting spots to athletes during recruiting trips, but many express that you exhibit some skills that lead them to believe that you could be a starter for their team. If this is the case, then keep putting in the work. It is important that you have someone you can talk to about these things so that you do not feel alone through the process.

Many athletes, especially track athletes, can find themselves plagued with injuries when a new training plan is put in place. It is important that you let the training staff know if you are having pain or experiencing discomfort with new exercises or lifts. There are also times when you do need to "suck it up," stop complaining, and just trust that your coaches and trainers know what they are doing. There is a difference between soreness and pain and you are the only one who can make that call. Remember to communicate with everyone in a respectful manner. Much like your professors and coaches, trainers have put in many long years to get certified as athletic trainers and you do not want them to feel as if you are telling them that they do not know how to do their jobs. Be respectful of their craft.

New teammates can also be a challenge. You spent many years developing relationships with your high school teammates and none of them may be with you as you continue on in your sport. You do not need to be best friends with all of your teammates; however, there will be ones that you get along with better than others. Even though you may not be best friends with all of your teammates, you will practice together, sweat together, shower together, lift weights together, share a locker room, and spend many hours a day together. You simply need to find teammates that have similar values and goals as yourself. Ultimately you are all working toward the same goal: to be better than your opponents and win.

What many athletes do find is that several of their teammates will be their best friends for the rest of their lives. You will share many things together: wins, losses, pain, happiness, and stories that you will never forget. This is one of the reasons why athletes are so bonded—because you have shared highs and lows, victories and defeats.

You will find that there are greater expectations on you both athletically and academically. Depending on what level you are competing at, many coaches lose their jobs if they are not successful on the field, in the pool, or on the court. This is their job and how they support themselves and their families, so they expect more from you so that you all can be successful.

Just as your coaches will have higher expectations of you, so will your professors. This is not high school anymore and you may face some transition issues with your academics. College professors, unlike your high school teachers, may not immediately know that you are a member of an athletic team. Many times in high school you could just get up and leave early from class or miss the class altogether without saying a word to your teacher. This would not be a good approach to take in college. As mentioned before, make sure that you are communicating in a respectful manner to your professor, who is your academic coach for a specific class. Don't make assumptions that they know you are an athlete and need to leave for travel or competition. Remind them repeatedly and often about your commitments to your team or sport. Don't expect them to make accommodations for you. If you will be missing classes, give them some options. Ask them if you can turn your assignment in before you leave or take the exam prior to your team travel. If proctors travel with you, then let your advisor and professor know that you may be able to take the test on the road if they are comfortable with this arrangement. Your transition will be much smoother if this communication happens on a regular basis.

Another transition that you may face is that college work is often different than high school work. High school tends to be a lot of memorization; college/university work requires much more complex thinking. Many English professors in college will not particularly care what position you take on an argumentative paper as long as you support your ideas with facts.

You may also find that your classes are not all bunched together like in high school. There are not six or seven periods in college. You may be only taking three or four classes spread out through the mornings and evenings. It is not abnormal for students in college to start at 7:00 A.M. and not finish until 8:00 P.M. Make sure that you use your time in between classes wisely.

This may be your first time away from home and living in a new environment can be challenging. You will have greater social freedoms and you may experience greater peer pressure as well. If you want to excel in your sport, then you will have to make some difficult choices when it comes to your free time. Will you go out and party with friends, sit at home and play video games, or take advantage of the time you have during the day so that work does not pile up for you after practice? Use your daily schedule or planner to achieve your goals each day, so that you can put the time and effort into your sport and not have your grades suffer. Don't forget to take some time for yourself as well. If you do choose to go party with your friends, then try to make responsible decisions. If you have practice the next day, you certainly do not want to feel terrible during that time.

If you are at a four-year university, many of you may be considered a "special admit." This means that you did not meet the regular admissions criteria, but because of your talent and ability as an athlete the university has allowed you to be admitted. Being a "special admit" is not a bad thing; it is a chance for you to take advantage of a unique opportunity. Surprising to many, athletes graduate at a higher rate than the regular student population even with all the "special admissions."

If you are a special admit or just feel as if you are not capable of competing in the classroom with other students, remember that you have the skills to be successful. Rely on your academic success team and communicate with them about your anxieties and fears.

STUDENT PROFILE

Julie is a first-year college student who earned a scholarship for a Division I women's soccer program. She was an excellent high school student-athlete who lettered three years for her soccer team and finished in the 10 percent of her graduating class academically. Everyone on her high school campus knew her and she had received countless accolades throughout her high school career. As her first year of college approached, she began experiencing some unexpected anxiety. Here is her story:

When I first got to college I had so much anxiety and I felt overwhelmed. I wasn't so concerned about my academics because I had always done well in school. I was more concerned about how I was going to deal with a new coach, new practice routine, and new teammates. I was a four-year starter on the varsity team in high school and I had created such good friendships with my teammates and coaches. My parents went to every game and now they were a long way away and would only be able to come out a few times a year. School hadn't even started yet and I already missed home.

I didn't want anyone to know that I was homesick because in athletics I was always taught to not show weakness and crying was a weakness to me. Our team had to report to school in early August and school did not start until the end of August. Myself and two other freshmen lived at one of the upperclassmen's house until the dorms opened two weeks later. It was hard to find private time to talk with my parents and friends, so I texted more than I talked. The first few days of practice and living on my own were really weird and it is hard to describe it now, but I didn't sleep well even though I was incredibly tired from our workouts. Our team would condition in the mornings and then come back in the afternoons for practice.

The times I did talk with my parents we talked about practice, the coach, the other women on the team and how I was doing with the team. After about a week I finally broke down on the phone with my mom and told her I didn't know if I wanted to stay because it was hard living with different people and I was so tired all the time. My mom encouraged me to stick it out for a few more weeks and if I still felt like I wanted to come home then I could. I decided to stick it out and I am sure glad that I did.

As I got to know many of the other girls on the team we started to talk more and our friendship developed; I trusted them a bit more and started to talk about more personal things. I was so surprised to hear the other freshmen on the team were feeling the same way I was and many of the second-, third-, and fourth-year students had experienced the same feelings. This really made me feel so much better and after two weeks I wasn't as tired and I had started to form some real friendships with these women on my team. It was so refreshing to know that I was not the only one who felt this way.

We started to talk about classes. A few of the second-year students had taken the same classes that I would be in for the fall term and they talked with me about what to expect in class. When I moved into the dorms, my roommate was another woman on the soccer team and we had gotten to know each other very well. A few of the other women were in a dorm just a few buildings away and we would visit each other all the time. I have met some other friends on my floor as well and other athletes that compete in other sports and we go to each other's games now. It is so much fun.

I can't believe that I even considered going home, now that I am so happy here and have made so many friends. I cook, I clean, I do my own laundry, I get my classwork done, and I am the starting left halfback for the soccer team.

I still talk to my parents about twice a week, but I have grown up so much and realize that the discomfort I felt at first was just part of the process. I was comfortable in high school and had a routine. I just needed to establish a similar routine in college. I can say that if I wouldn't have had teammates to talk to things may have turned out different, but I have so much in common with most of the women on the team. I am not best friends with everyone on the team, but we all get along and really appreciate each other.

I am really looking forward to the years to come and what I am going to experience while I am here.

Julie was the typical "big fish in a small pond" at her high school. Her experience with college athletics is not out of the ordinary. Fears, anxieties, and questioning your place in a new environment can be challenging. Once she was able to develop some relationships with her teammates she realized that she was not alone.

Take the time to try to develop some relationships with your teammates or others on your campus that can help make your transition to college a bit easier. Small fish in a big pond are hard to find unless they are going out of their way to get some attention. Don't be afraid to go out of your way to try to establish some meaningful relationships that will help with your transition.

WHAT AM I GOING TO DO WHEN ATHLETICS IS OVER?

Athletics are great and competing in your sport for as long as you can should be a goal of every athlete, but everyone knows that athletics does not always equate to the real world. You don't show up to a training room an hour before you go to work and get rubbed down before clocking in at 8:00 A.M. Nobody stretches out the regional manager for Enterprise before he goes to work for the day. As I am writing this supplement for student-athletes, Pearson Publishing is not hooking me up with a bunch of free "swag" with Pearson Pride all over it. You will be responsible for washing your own work clothes (no equipment manager at PepsiCo). If you get injured on the job, everything doesn't stop until you are carted out of the office. No one standing on the sideline with Gatorade ready to squirt in your mouth. And for those of you who get great fan attendance, 80,000 people will not show up to cheer for you as you are trying to close a sales deal.

Hopefully this does not come as a surprise to you, but you need to understand that athletics is just one phase of your life. You are obviously very good at your sport, but you will need to start thinking about a plan B. Appreciate the "swag," priority enrollment, trainers, coaches, strength and conditioning coaches, free books, and scholarship checks, because it will come to an end at some point. Even if you do get to compete professionally, a very minute percentage of athletes make a living at it for any extended period of time. Even for those who do make it and achieve a living wage, it does not last long. There is a very small window for you to make money in your sport. According to Kurt A. David (Sport and American Society, 2010), "60% of NBA players are broke five years after they leave the game and 75% of NFL players are broke within two years of leaving the game." There is nothing better than making money in your sport, but the truth is that relying on your sport for long-term financial security is a losing bet. College is a great time to work hard and maximize your athletic potential, yet it is also a time to explore other passions and figure out what your other interests are in life.

Here are two more sources of statistics for you to think about:

According to *The Big Payoff: Educational Attainment and Synthetic Estimates of Work-Life Earnings*, high school graduates can expect to earn $1.2 million over a lifetime and college graduates can expect to earn $2.1 million over a lifetime. This is almost a million dollars more over a lifetime.

A new Pew Research Center analysis (2011), using Census Bureau data, estimates that the typical adult with a bachelor's degree (but no further education) will earn $1.42 million over a 40-year career, compared with $777,000 for a typical high school graduate. That $650,000 difference narrows somewhat to $550,000, according to the analysis, after factoring in the expenses of going to college and the four years of potential earnings that college graduates give up while they are in school. Regardless of how much credibility you give to statistics, it seems clear that you can earn in excess of one half a million dollars over a lifetime by earning your bachelor's degree.

Give yourself some credit for being a stud athlete right now, but also appreciate the opportunity that you have been given and capitalize on the benefit of being at a two- or four-year institution right now. Seize the moment and use this time to explore what other passions you may have besides athletics. Many athletes don't take the time to think about different areas of their lives because they are an athlete and this is their identity. There is nothing

Start thinking about your transition from your athletic career to your professional career.

wrong with identifying yourself as an athlete first, but think about how you may describe yourself besides as a swimmer, golfer, football player, baseball player, tennis player, or the like.

- Are you a high school graduate?
- Are you outgoing or an introvert?
- Are you someone who values strong friendships?
- Do you enjoy speaking in public?
- Are you reliable?
- What subject areas do you like to learn about?
- Do you read outside of school? If so, what types of books?

If someone were to ask you, "What are you passionate about?" and you couldn't mention your sport, what would you say? College is the time to start to answer such a question.

Transitional issues coming into college/university were mentioned previously, but there will be some transitional issues when your eligibility has expired and you are not required to be at practice, weights, and games regularly. Start thinking about what this will be like for you. By no means do we suggest that you should not work as hard as you can in your sport. If you have dreams and aspirations of making millions in your sport, then by all means chase those dreams. However, when your college experience comes to an end you should have some alternatives to support yourself and your family. Don't put all your eggs in one basket. Life is a game of adjustments and right now you have time to work on your offense and defense. Remember you have "mad skills."

LET'S SUMMARIZE THE GAME

It is our hope that after reading this you feel that you possess some extraordinary skills. You simply need to hone these skills and make them work for you in everyday life. Academics is not the only area you can apply these tools. When you communicate with different individuals in your personal life, make sure that you are aware of who your audience is and communicate accordingly. If you would like to set some career goals for yourself, use the activities in this supplement to help you get there. If you are struggling to balance all of your social obligations, develop a time management strategy. Build relationships and network so that you are building a success team that will help you be a winner beyond your college experience.

College is a wonderful time in young people's lives and athletics adds to this experience. It also adds to the overall learning experience. Take a look at your college or university's learning objectives and see how many you can apply to your sport. Take advantage of the opportunity that you have been given and make it work to your advantage. Life is a game, much like your sport. It has rules and outcomes. It has ups and downs and bumps in the road, but when you look back at the overall experience it should be one that you are very proud of and cherish. There are many people on your campus that can help you achieve your goals and dreams, both athletically and academically. They are your teammates too, and they can set you up for a winning shot or to achieve your personal best. Build relationships with these people and communicate effectively with them throughout your college journey.